I0644517

A Black Kite

A Black Kite

Selected Poems of Kim Jong-Gil

Translated by
Brother Anthony of Taizé
and Kim Jong-Gil

MERWIN
MA
ASIA

MerwinAsia
Portland, Maine

MerwinAsia
59 West St., Unit 3W,
Portland, ME 04102
USA

www.merwinasia.com

MERWIN
ASIA

The translation and publication of this book
were made possible by the generosity
of the Literature Translation Institute of Korea

Library of Congress Control Number: 2017908386

ISBN 978-1-937385-35-4 (pbk)
ISBN 978-1-937385-45-3 (cloth)

Printed in the United States of America

Cover and interior design by Lucian Burg, LU Design Studios, Portland, ME
www.ludesignstudios.com

The paper used in this publication
meets the minimum requirementsof the American National Standard for
Information Services—
Permanence of Paper for Printed Library Materials,
ANSI/NISO Z39/48-1992

Distributed by the University of Hawai'i Press

CONTENTS

In Memoriam: Kim Jong-Gil (1926–2017)

Kim Jong-Gil died on April 1, 2017, only a few days after the death of his wife, in his ninety-first year. He was born in 1926 in the region of Andong, in Jirye-dong Village in the county which was then known as Gilanmyeon (now Imdongmyeon). He was one of Korea's most senior literary figures. His mother died when he was only two years old. In his early childhood he was cared for by his father and grandmother and especially his great-grandfather, who was a noted scholar of the old Confucian tradition. He began to learn Chinese characters from his great-grandfather almost before he could walk. He studied in a teachers' training school in Daegu, the Daegu Sabeom Simsanggwa, and from 1940 for several years he helped edit a literary coterie magazine there. In 1945, after the liberation of Korea from Japanese rule, he entered the humanities section of Haehwa College (Haehwa jeonmun hakgyo) in Seoul. There he formed a literary club with other students which began to produce its own magazine.

Having begun to write poems, he won the 1947 Spring Literary Award of the *Gyeonghyang Sinmun* (a daily newspaper), marking the start of his official career as a published poet. In the spring of the same year he transferred schools and entered the English Department of Korea University. There he came under the influence of Professor Lee In-su, the first Korean to have graduated in English Literature from the University of London, a gifted translator, who introduced him to T. S. Eliot's "Wasteland." He graduated in 1950 and during the Korean War (1950–53) he served as an interpreter. From 1953 he taught in Daegu Technical High School and also lectured in the College of Education of Gyeongbok University; in 1954 he was appointed full-time lecturer at Gyeongbok University and in the same year published a volume of translations of twentieth-century English poetry. After two years at Cheonggu University from 1956, he became assistant professor in the Department of English Language and Literature at Korea University in 1958.

In 1960 he was able to go to England, where he spent a year studying at Sheffield University under the guidance of the celebrated critic William Empson. During this time he met T. S. Eliot and other well-known writers and critics. Returning to Korea University, he continued his academic career. In 1969 he published his first collection of poems, "Christmas." In the autumn that year he visited the United States where he met celebrated poets including Robert Lowell. In the following years he lectured, published critical studies, and served for several years as the University Librarian. In 1983 he paid another visit to England, where he met noted literary critics including Christopher Ricks and A. Alvarez, and in the following year he was able to spend a study year at the University of Cambridge. In 1986 he celebrated his sixtieth birthday by publishing a volume of prose writings, a survey of modern English-language poetry, a second collection of his own poems, "Yellow Dust," and a volume of poetic theory.

Throughout his career, he translated into English poems by a considerable number of contemporary Korean poets. Those translations were published here and there in various Korean journals but were never published as a separate collection. A selection of those translations was included in the anthology "The Colors of Dawn" published by Manoa (University of Hawai'i) in 2016. In 1987, Anvil Press (London) published a volume of his English translations of Korean Classical Chinese poetry, "Slow Chrysanthemums." In 1988 he became President of the Korean Poets' Association. He participated in a number of international gatherings, and so met Seamus Heaney in Kyoto in 1990. In 1991 a volume of his selected poems was published, followed by a collection of his English-language literary essays, "The Darling Buds of May." Throughout his life, he participated in groups which met to compose poetry in the Traditional Classical Chinese forms.

He retired from Korea University in 1992, after which he was free to travel and give papers at various international conferences around the world. In 1993 he was elected a member of the Korean Academy of Arts. In 1996 he was given the Inchon Award. His third collection of poems, "An Evening Primrose," appeared in 1997 and in 1998 he received the Korean government's Silver Order of Merit for Culture. In 2000 his English translations of the poems of Kim Chun-su were published in the United States. In 2003 a volume of German translations of a selection of his poems was published in Germany. In 2005 he received the Gosan Literary Award. In 2008 he published another collection of poems, "Gleaning at Dusk," and a Spanish translation of some of his poems appeared in Mexico. In 2009 he published a collection of essays about his encounters with celebrated international writers and also received the Manhae Award. In 2011 he published the poetry collection "Those Things," and in 2013 he published a volume of his selected poems, "The Kite," which is here translated into English. A number of the poems had already been translated by the poet in years past, and in 2016 he read through Brother Anthony's translations of the other poems, indicating corrections or improvements to be made. To the very end he was a lucid and scrupulous poet, translator and scholar.

Kim Jong-gil explained that the pressure of his work as an academic meant that he had very little time to write his own poetry. The poems in this collection represent those which he considered his finest from throughout his long career. The year 2017 marked the seventieth anniversary of his recognition as a poet. This volume is dedicated to his memory.

—Brother Anthony

A Black Kite

Rapids

I cross the rapids,

following the uphill road
on the first day of school

having spent the summer
without even once having
the water in the rapids touch me,

leaving the street,
hot as a sandbank,

as I cross September air currents the hue of balloon flowers

shoals of silvery minnows
sparkling like shoals of silvery minnows

the songs of morning insects in the grass . . .

Christmas

Beside a glowing charcoal fire
in a dark room, all alone,

my elderly grandmother
was keeping watch over a pitifully fading young life.

At last Father returned home through the snow
bringing medicine;

Ah, those red cornelian cherries
Father had picked after plowing through the snow . . .

I was a baby animal,
my fever-flushed cheeks being silently rubbed
with the cool hem of young Father's coat.

From time to time snow beat at the back door.
I have a feeling that that evening was Christmas Eve.

And suddenly I have reached the age
my father was then.

That being something irrecoverable from long ago, in a town
with Christmas drawing near
those welcome memories from the past come dropping down.

If I suddenly feel Father's cool coat hem
on my sorrowful thirty-year-old brow

is that because the red cornelian cherries picked in the snow
are still flowing, melted, in my blood?

On New Year's Morning

The sun comes and goes
in the constant cold,

but the new year has somehow to be greeted warmly.

Below the ice, fish are still breathing
and green water parsley buds
are dreaming of spring days.

The new year has to be greeted with endurance
and with a little dreaming.

I spent this morning
before a glass of warm liquor
and a bowl of soup,

so I should think that is plenty
and feel grateful.

The world
is rough and cruel
but still it's worth living in;

we should think about being better and wiser
since today we are one year older.

Though one year goes
in the bitter cold
and another comes,

just as we see pretty teeth emerging
through the gums of babies,

so we should welcome the new year.

Spring Mud

The womens' university had cream-colored buildings.

The mud stuck to the soles of shoes did not fall off readily.

The end of the suitably gasping hill path

was a greenish barley field . . .

There was a sound of a white tennis ball bouncing somewhere.

It was too early for cuckoos to be singing

but up on the hill

newly entering students were chattering like skylarks.

Middle Age

The seasons are always guests ushered in by rain . . .
it may be a ruddy-cheeked boy, a sunburned youth,
someone middle-aged mined by melancholy,
or a grizzle-browed old man,
but it is always the same guest, not a different one,

Beyond the bead curtain of raindrops hanging from the eaves
how many time have I welcomed that guest?
This middle-aged traveler mined by melancholy—
what ushered him in previously,
as a ruddy-cheeked boy, a sunburned youth
lingering beneath some house's eaves?

If chill autumn rain drizzles down hastily,
one day white snow flurries will sprinkle the brow!
Now, just like that ruddy-cheeked boy lingering
beyond the bead-curtain of rain-drops,
will this traveler never again flush with childlike cheeks
and linger one day outside some window?

Lonely Height

For Mount Bukhan
to recover its full height,
we have to wait till winter comes.

We have to wait
till a winter morning dawns after a night of snow
when only such high peaks as Baegundae or Insubong stand
covered with light snow as if with thin makeup,

while the rest of the mountain remains the colour
of cold Indian ink.

For Mount Pukhan to recover
its lonely height which does not reveal itself
in the fresh green or the turning of leaves,
or in the fog rising along the valleys,

not even when deep snow covers the whole mountain,
but is diminished even at the touch of a rosy sunbeam,

we have to wait till a winter morning dawns
when only Paegundae and Insubong stand
covered with light snow.

Near a Mountaintop

Mist is flowing irregularly
over the afternoon's Ant-Back Ridge.

If we choose a patch of grass and sit down,
it is bound to hold prickly thistles; in the mist a few cows
are looking at us with docile faces like the Holy Family.

In Jeju City oleanders were blooming heatedly
near the mountaintop a late autumn wind is rising.

Burying the setting sun on the stone walls of toothbrush-like
    Crown Peak,
darkness buries Yongjingak Valley.

On Mount Halla in July
the streams and the chirping of insects are merely chill.

Baekrok Lake where it seems a lost calf fell in and drowned
the morning of fearfully blue waves,
walking on round the crater, as we turn toward Seoguipo,
a suddenly rushing sea breeze
comes twisting white round the gaunt stone pillars of the south
    face.
Not mist, now, but clouds.

Blooming in those clouds, beds of mountain flowers,
and over them a flock of yellow butterflies is turning.

Grading

You were on the tall side, weren't you?
Your posture was always bolt upright, wasn't it?

I set about grading the end-of-term exam papers
after having seen your name and photo
in a newspaper article about a bus accident.

On the report card you would never see
I copied, writing clearly,
a grade just short of 90 points.

As I looked round the memorial exhibition prepared by your
 comrades
I realized how much you had also grown up in poetry.

"In an August garden" where you said "roses are lighting lamps"
you stand, tall and upright.

One woman among those graduating,
you said, "I often read my palm,"
and now you stand there alone as ever.

At Hahoi Village

The name means a stream flows round the village
and today still that stream is flowing.

Has time too just gone on flowing away like the stream?
No. No, it's piled on the mossy tiles of the old houses
and today after the summer rain is drying in the hot sunlight.

And it is growing in the shiny leaves of a mulberry tree
on the site of a demolished house,
reviving in the coughing of the elderly grandson at
    Yangjindang.

In the green quinces on the few trees
in the back garden of Chunghyodang, the former home of
    Master Seoae,

and on the site where an exhibition hall is being built
at the expense of the Office of Cultural Properties,
it is being reconstituted.

Autumn Chill

Today in this inland city,
famed for its heat,
under the influence of a typhoon
cool breezes have been blowing all day.
It has been a week since I heard of a friend's death
and as I walk along this street again,
the chaos of Chuseok having passed,
that friend is walking with me.
I feel that occasionally his fearfully broad shoulders
strike against mine.
His lifetime, just forty-seven years,
was like this city's sultry heat.
Still, what can be the reason why his life, which was not long,
but was particularly full of hardships and pain,
feels to those of us who were close to him
like today's weather, with cool breezes blowing?
The main street of this city with its million and more
inhabitants
today seems quite empty,
while we who are walking along are somehow feckless like the
breeze.
Yet, as we talk about him,
we sometimes laugh.
He grew increasingly gaunt
then as the heat he had to endure at the end was decreasing
his life, too, ended.
This inland city which he has left for ever,
the familiar northern hills veiled in clouds . . .
this year the autumn chill seems to have arrived particularly
early.

A Bicycle

On a downward slope I accelerate.
I just have to keep my feet on the pedals.

But I have to maintain my balance.
And something might suddenly come dashing out.
I need to be ready for that kind of unexpected event.

Still, like this, a peaceful downward slope,
sunlight breaking and bouncing off the spokes,
the bell ringing *ting-a-ling*.

The bottom of the hill growing dark,
though still, ultimately expecting to fall off,
entrusting myself to inertia, quite refreshing,

I go rolling down the hill in the autumn sunset,
barely keeping my balance,
gently applying the brakes.

Evening Sun

One year in late autumn in the afternoon one day
I was in an express train heading for the South-East.

As the train was passing Suwon,
the brilliant evening sun reflected in Seoho Lake
shone so dazzling straight through the train window.

I turned into a sightless worm
burrowing into an apple,
a golden delicious.

The meadows where harvest was over, too,
the scrub where the leaves had fallen, too, the houses, too,
by that golden glow all found themselves inside ripe pulp.

Flowering Plum

Every year as the new year begins
without fail plum blossom blooms on the potted tree.
This year the first bud blossomed on the first day of the lunar
year.

As if wanting to announce that the new year had come,
as if keeping some kind of promise,
a bud blossoming on New Year's Day!

The black trunk that seemed dry and dead,
the parched thin twigs
were still alive after all!

As if to say it had not forgotten, not forgotten
that I could not throw it out so long as it was alive,
plum blossom blooms without fail.

Outside, snow is falling.
As if to announce that the plum had bloomed,
outside, plum-blossom-hued snow is falling,

The Southward Path

The other day, all through the afternoon, peach blossom
was being soaked crimson in drizzle.

Now in every fresh green valley
a few paulownias are blossoming purple.

As the moon passes from the fourth month to the fifth
how the landscape changes!

This path, the homeward path, southward path,
changing with the seasons, the landscape along the path.

With age, more frequent journeys home,
with age, new roadside landscapes.

Evening Star

Nowadays in Seoul
it is hard to find any stars in the night sky

When I was a child in the countryside,
evening stars even used to shine
in the puddles outside the village.

In those days the water and even the wind were clear.
The evening stars reflected in the puddles
used to quiver like wild-flower petals.

In the puddles
the sky would grow dark
and a breeze rise.

Dried Pollack

On the way home, feeling quite weary,
I got off the bus and entered an alley.

In front of fruit shops, vegetable shops, fish shops,
women sitting at the roadside selling sundae-sausage or bean-
    sprouts,
men with carts frying corn or spinning cotton candy,

Various ways of earning a living—
Carrying in my hands books and chalk from the classroom,
chattering away non-stop, at times mixing in erudite foreign
    words.

Earning a salary, receiving bonuses, I am living
by excited clamoring, like those bold-faced salesmen
shouting the praises of things that are nothing special.

If manpower too is merchandise,
surely I too am merchandise?
Facing retirement, that's merchandise on the verge of becoming
    junk.

That gaunt dried pollack stuck on a skewer
left over in a fish shop.
In those bleary eyes it cannot close, limpid,

the winter sky,
the winter sky at sunset
with an icy wind rising.

An Evening Primrose

My home village left nearly empty
at the completion of the Imha Dam,

The road newly pierced through
the cindery slopes I used to cross on my way to market
curved like a banded snake.

Passing over a 30 *li* road,
treading with my eyes the hillside's bitter clay hue
wounded by a rattling van

Only evening primroses blooming abundantly along the
  roadsides
welcomed me instead of the villagers.

A Black Kite
—In Andong

Sick without being ill,
like the rice for false offerings at the Andong Dam Folk Village,
let's not write such things as poems.

Across the river, in the roof furrows of Imcheonggak mansion
still the north wind from Manchuria is blowing
and even at midday unexpected frost falls.

Truth is not a product of the warm place on an ondol floor
but something reflected in a frosted window,
the winter rainbow of martyred Yuksa!

Now there is nothing like the stork that used slowly to fly.
Lighting a fire in the landscape embedded in ice,
today again in the blazing evening sky,

Ruffling its feathers
as it braves the icy wind
a single kite.

Twilight Glow

As we move into Siberian airspace
the afternoon sun that has been moving with the plane
finally begins to pass in front.

Lake Baikhal should be somewhere to the north.
Over the vast continent twilight is spreading
not one human lamp strikes the eye.

Even as we pass above the Urals
there is no real sundown in the air,
only above the horizon bent like a bow

as we fly on and on, a crimson glow,
binding up the wounds of the black ground
a blood-soaked strip of bandage.

Russia, Finland, Sweden,
Denmark, the Netherlands, then England—
the European sky the plane is passing through

is everywhere bleeding.

Translated by Kim Jong-Gil

Five Thousand Years

Did you miss your step,
while chasing after a stag?
Though not the hell of sizzling brimstone,
thirty fathoms of snow must have sufficed for your death.

After five thousand years,
you resurrected magnificently in flesh:
the perfect limbs of a man about forty,
lungs thick with soot from bonfires in a cave.

It might have been warm for you,
in the blue ice of a glacier near Innsbruck.
That last Alpine sunset that you saw, as your eyes
closed in the breeze coming through the pines of Tyrol.

Were those five thousand years
as short as an afternoon's nap to you?
What shout did you raise at your last moment?

*Note: The subject of this poem is a mummy discovered in 1991
in an ice field in the Alps near Innsbruck and identified
as that of a man of about five thousand years ago.*

Translated by Kim Jong-Gil

Back Home

Along the stream in front of my former village,
the clumps of willow rooted in the gravel,
the rows of poplars in the sand have all vanished.

The newly made Imha Lake
is spread with multiple watery scales
reflecting the autumn sunlight.

They say our country changes every ten years
and while it has changed seven times
I have grown old traveling far from home.

My home village has been submerged,
to that extent our country has changed,
so that I and the former landscape cannot recognize each other.

Half an evening spent gazing down at the site of the old house
where I was born, spent my childhood,
that valley, early subsets of late autumn evenings.

Finally back, from the rearward mountain ridge,
I gaze blankly at the lake before the village.
Like seeing someone unfamiliar, an unfamiliar landscape.

In Seokpo

After forty years, I visited Seokpo
which was my mother's home.
Together with a group of people from Seoul
making a literary tour.

Dilapidated old tiled houses standing in lines
with almost no sign of anyone living in them.

Beside the former home of the novelist Yi Mun-Yol rose
Yu-u-dang, home of the head of my mother's family, into
    which
my uncle, the poet the late Yi Byong-gak had been adopted,
    where
the wooden board on which the name of the house was carved
still hung above the faded wooden porch of the men's quarters.

My former mother's home had a new owner,
it seemed to have been repaired, looked less dilapidated
but the main gate hung shut.

The house where Mother was born, grew up,
and died at the young age of twenty-two.
After which, whenever I went visiting during vacations
Grandmother used to weep tears afresh.

As I peep from the alley at the door
of the east-facing room where Grandmother used to live,
I start to return to childhood.

In the weak late-autumn sunshine
in that childhood alley overgrown with nettles,
caught among the other people, I was walking alone.

Mount Cheongryang in Autumn

Do mountains also grow thin in autumn?
The chill cliffs of Mount Cheongryang soaring
into the deep blue sky,

The broad-leaved trees
mixed in among the green pines
were merely tinged a pale brown

while really bright autumn colors
were restricted to the ivy climbing up the cliffs
or the leaves of the lacquer trees.

Already more than brightly thin,
a middle-aged scholar, starting to be coldly thin,

Mount Cheongryang in autumn.

Niagara

Before a resonant torrent
that shakes the axis of the world
do people grow so much more generous?

Merely seen
from the the top of the hill, holding the rail,
the quantity is not a problem.

Satisfaction only seems to come
after boarding a boat and emerging
after a trip around the foot of the falls
drenched in spray.

The name of the boat is "Maid of the Mists"
and that bridge high up there is "Rainbow Bridge;"
before such a spectacle even pragmatists all turn into poets.

In Manhattan

Returning after several decades,
the distinctive Manhattan skyline
is unchanged, then and now.

Then it was early October, now mid-June,
and above the dazzling green verdure of Central Park
golden sunlight is shattering.

But already twenty years have passed
since the poet Robert Lowell died,
whom I visited then in his home.

My contemporary, Allen Ginsberg,
who came to Seoul seven years ago,
passed away last April.

There is nobody left who is glad to see me
in the crowded Metropolitan Museum
or the alleys beside Rockefeller Center.

Back in Manhattan after a long absence—
one silent Sunday afternoon
with the golden sunlight all the sadder.

Beholding Tai-shan

I know nothing of the geological movements long ago in East
  Asia
but I reckon that China and Korea were originally joined
  together.
The way the Liaotung Peninsula and the Shandong Peninsula
  stick out
suggests that, while the indentations of the Korean west coast are
  striking.

But an even more convincing proof
is the texture of the white granite exposed on Tai-shan,
so very similar to that of Mount Bukhan!

The skin of Tai-shan glimpsed
between the green pine trees
is exactly the same as that of Mount Bukhan.

Likewise the white clouds poised on the peaks
are the least bit different from those
on Baegundae and Insubong.

That is why the words of Lao-tzu, Confucius, Mencius,
who were born in the region overlooked by Tai-shan
were sure to sound not the least strange to our ears.

At Cambridge

No matter when you come,
there is nothing that has changed
on King's Parade. The street is exactly as it was:

St. John's, Trinity, Caius, Clare, King's,
the college buildings of worn and faded
stone or brickwork.

Do even knowledge and wisdom, accumulated pile on pile,
turn into such solid towers, gathering moss
and revealing delicate, antique hues?

On this street where only the autumnal ivy leaves
and the fine green lawns belong to growth and death,
where space and time are one,

you feel no distinction between morning and evening,
nor the transition from season to season. Here,
you hold your breath in the timeless quietude.

Translated by Kim Jong-Gil

Dawn Moon

Just half a year
since the poet Yi Seong-seon left us,
who took Mount Seorak for his universe.

At dawn on the day set for the unveiling
of his memorial stone in the precincts of Baekdam temple
which he often visited,

Strolling alone in those precincts
I look up at the dawn moon
now in its nineteenth day,

as in life,
his freckled

face

on his way up after washing
in the cold water
of the stream in front of the temple.

Yellow Dust and Cherry Blossom and . . .

Yellow dust and cherry blossom and a dawning sky . . .
nowadays my daily routine begins with such things.

If despite the long spring drought
a little rain happens to fall,
the sound of the stream is well worth the hearing.

There are times when a thread-like
trickle of water hangs between rocks
at some point along the valley.

One expanse of nature's beauty spreading anew each morning
and at the end of the path climbing up the valley,
standing quiet, a hermitage.

Waking at Dawn

Old folks
enjoy no dawn sleep.

If I wake too early,
though I try to get back to sleep again,
while I hover in between time passes quickly.

Ringing in the ears of old folks waking early
a sound of streams flowing, rain dripping—
but if I open a window it's not raining.

All the disgusting things about growing old
seem but the clouds of the sky when the horizon fades
to Yeats gazing down at the hour of death in his early sixties.

I wonder if I am not gazing at that hour on my dawn bed,
while the time I enjoy in this world flows by
roaring like rapids in my ears.

A Yellow Dog Groan

After spending his life as a hunter outside the East Gate
with a yellow dog, he became prime minister
and therefore met a violent death,

and it is said that as he was dying, regretfully he wished
he had not become prime minister
but had gone on living as a hunter with a yellow dog.

The groan of Li Si of the Chinese Qin dynasty,
a yellow dog groan.

But his skill with the brush was outstanding,
he was celebrated as a great calligrapher with Wang Xizhi,
that unfortunate, extraordinary man of many parts.

I am neither a hunter, nor a prime minister nor a famed
    calligrapher,
but I too live outside the East Gate of Seoul
and nowadays I go for walks with a yellow dog.

I stroll up the valley to Baengnyeon temple in the early
    morning
with no misfortune, nothing extraordinary,
ruminating over my worthless life.

Husband and Wife

On top of a dark stove
or on an old table,
it is only when they are caught in a chance gleam of evening
sunlight

that a pair of old bowls
briefly shows their true appearance.

Whether made of brass or pottery or earthenware,
together day after day for more than fifty years,
going about together, despite being stained, toothless

Dishes or bowls
that have always to be together to feel right.

Giving birth to no few children, bringing them up,
marrying them off, sending them away,
until now just the two remain.

Occasionally glancing at one another's thin white hair,
crows-feet round the eyes,
perhaps because they cannot break together,
even though one breaks,
idly smiling at one another and meditating,

The day's remaining sunlight beyond the window,
an unseasonable dewdrop quivering in the sunlight.

Looking up at White Cloud Terrace

On Li Po's Jinling's Phoenix Terrace
a phoenix played a while then vanished but

On our Mount Bukhan's White Terrace
white clouds play a while then vanish,
then after vanishing they return again and play.

Paired with brawny Insu Peak,
guardian of Seoul North and East,
how many millions of years have they endured, standing there?

The better matched with the white granite skin,
irregularly stopping, going, returning,
two or three white clouds,

Now gleaming on your brow,
dying it a rosy hue,
sunlight of the new millennium's first morning!

Perhaps a millennium to you is merely half a day?
Looking up at you, we perceive eternity.

On the first morning of the new millennium
with one white cloud passing in a leisurely way,
I see eternity.

Pain

People like flowers,
but they fail to realize
at the end of how much pain they bloom.

I too had to reach my present age
before I realized that.

It was only when I observed from early spring
in the heads of azaleas,
the tedious endurance

as the flower buds pitifully, pitifully,
squeezed out the green sweat-like sap
that I came to realize that.

The Poet Kim Chun-su in Intensive Care

Ever since you were a child, you
lived in a different world from other people.

Whether it was Tongyeong or Seoul or Tokyo,
you had your own sky, your own sea,
your own city space.

At the same time, within history that made a victim of you
you lived unfairly, awkwardly
as a stranger among strangers.

Now, for nearly three months, you have been lying
unconscious in a bed in intensive care.
Instead of your former customary morning walk,

completely cut off from the world,
at the height of self-alienation, attached to a respirator,
you are walking around the suburbs of life.

The Year I Turn Eighty

The face in the mirror changes with time.
The heart, still young, is the same as last year.
(Yeonam Bak Ji-won)

As Yeonam wrote, although we grow older,
what never changes
is our childhood heart.

Suddenly I am turning eighty but my heart
is still like a little boy
playing by the sea.

Not realizing that the sun is setting,
picking up sea shells,
spending time with baby crabs,

the day will come when suddenly
fierce waves will cover me
and my body will fall like a leaf.

A child,
paying no attention to such things,
immersed in play.

Still the sea is peaceful,
and in the sky, one, two,
stars begin to shine.

Sweeping Snow

Intending to sweep up the snow that fell earlier,
I went out into the still dark alley

But on the snow, white like a sheet of paper,
the marks of the bicycle tires, the shoes
of the newspaper boy, of the milkman are printed.

Just as though a worm had crawled past,
a crow gone speeding by with rapid steps,

Without those marks
the alley so prettily wrapped in snow
would be more beautiful, surely?

But in that case, why am I striving so hard
to brush away the alley's snow?

One evening in America's New Hampshire
poet Robert Frost, you stopped your sleigh
beside a wood as snow fell
and gazed at the snow piling up
in the "dark deep" wood.

Did you, too, not confess then,
'I have miles to go before I sleep,
miles to go before I sleep'?
Indeed, newspaper boy, milkman,
even worms and crows, and I
have miles to go before we sleep.

Before I sleep, I still have
some miles to go.

Wonderful Days

At a time without anything considered wonderful,
nowadays I come face to face with wonder
every morning.

If I go out into the garden early in the morning
in the clusters of roses in the flowerbed outside the window
ripen more fully day by day,

on the pines along the hillside trails
buds grow bigger
as though caught in the hand.

At this time every year why do my eyes focus afresh
on these things that are always just the same? At an age
when there is supposed to be nothing in the world to marvel at.

In Kyoto

By the pond called Mirror Pond
rises Kinkaku-ji
like a golden lotus.

Buried at the tips of the eaves
the evening sun.

Rough sand raked,
here and there rocks disposed like islands,
the rectangular rock garden in Ryoanji.

Dusk descending
on that garden.

After touring these two temples,
the essence of Japanese culture,
located three bus-stops from one another,

came the evening drinks smelling of fish
in the raw-fish chain restaurant Uotami.

Looking at a Persimmon Tree

The persimmon tree that has spent
some thirty years living in a corner of my garden
is having a barren year,
so only a few persimmons have ripened.
Still, more than fifty have ripened appetizingly
and hang in groups of two or three
at the ends of the branches.
The more the leaves fall the more they strike the eye.
Once frosts begin and all the leaves have fallen
I'll leave just a few for the magpies
and harvest all the rest.
My garden is all the land I own
and although gathering over forty persimmons there
is my entire harvest for this year,
I am more satisfied and delighted than any great landlord.
It alone is enough for me to enjoy abundance.

Climbing Taebaek Mountain

Spread over the floor of dried yellow grass,
the dark green leaves of dwarf bamboo,
and reeling at their tips,
platinum sunlight!

Cut, gaping tree trunks patched with cement,
at the end of half-withered branches,
still yew trees with haggard green leaves
are as yet old champions.

On ridges some fifteen hundred meters high
even sturdy oaks struggle against the gales.
Branches incline,
twisted like crippled limbs.

So I, who have endured
panting, barely putting one foot in front of another,
withstanding the world's storms through eighty years,

Now
what shape am I in?

In the Birthplace of Heo Nan-Seol-Heon

Beyond the sand-dunes
the drowsy spring sea is snoozing.

Bent-backed old pines
in place of the village elders
stand in sparse lines at the entrance to the neighborhood.

Even after entering through the front gate
there is not so much as a person's shadow in sight.
Every room's sliding door and shutters are closed.

Where have this house's talented children all gone?
Inside the wall where plum blossom is over,
on branches of two pink peaches
clusters of flowers dangle.

On Passing through Hanam

After a lunch of sliced meat and beef-bone soup at a restaurant
on the outskirts of Masan where Kim Chun-su used to live,
leaving Changwon where it seems the poet Bae Han-bong is
living,
passing Jinyeong, as we enter Hanam in the region of Milyang
I remember Yi Yu-gyeong's "Hanam Poems,"
as well as Yi Dal-hui's cycle of poems "Naktong River"
which won the Hankook Ilbo's Spring Literary Awards one
year.
The fine silk scarf wrapped round the neck of the old woman
who used to cross the river embracing the fierce storms—
but that was farther down the river, I think.
The bed of reeds where wild geese settle,
mentioned in that famous *Yeongnamru* poem, is not visible.
Only the Yeongnam pavilion still gazes from its cliff
out at the distant "blue mountains of the ocean."

Note: the last line echoes a line from the Yeongnamru *poem.*

Chiaroscuro

The house in Amsterdam
where Rembrandt is said to have lived for a while—
that narrow wooden staircase leading down from the upper
floor.

In Saint Petersburg
the wooden staircase in the house where Dostoyevsky once
lived
was narrow, too, with a thin bannister.

Sunlight happening to strike a dark screen—
sensing the intense chiaroscuro of Rembrandt, Master of
Light,
in Dostoyevsky's works, as I do,

Is that natural, or
is it merely my private fantasy?

Gilt-Bronze Pensive Bodhisattva, National Treasure No. 83

The right leg folded horizontally
with the ankle resting on the left knee,
the left hand clasping that ankle.

Is that a lotus blooming above the elbow resting on the thigh?
The three fingers of the right hand
slightly bent almost touching the cheek.

For a thousand and several hundred years
that selfsame poise, never wavering,
what is it pondering so intently?

Human suffering? Birth, old age, sickness, and death?
So far removed from such things,
that lovely, youthful, almost childlike face!

The Path up Mount Toham

When you reach the top of the path
winding its way up the side of Mount Toham
piercing the dark green foliage,

The East Sea comes in sight,
the tomb of King Munmu comes in sight.

Just before you leave the valley
the road branches toward Gampo,
and amidst the greenery along the road,

pink silk-tree or
crape myrtle flowers draw the gaze.

For a thousand leagues the orioles sing,
green and pink are in harmony,
as the poet Du Mu wrote in his landscape poems.

The Han River Today

Curving as though gouging out the middle of the Korean
 peninsula
then joining at Watersmeet, the South and North Han Rivers
flow past the Paldang dam then round the eastern corner of
 Seoul,
 the capital,
banks opening to south and north, a wide river bed
and bright sand banks spread wide.

Neither the Thames in London nor the Seine in Paris,
not the Potomac in Washington, nor the East River and
 Hudson
 in New York,
neither the Edo River nor the Sumida River of Tokyo in nearby
 Japan,
offers scenes as bright and gentle as our Han River.

That's not all! Here and there along its banks are a dozen or so
pavilions with splendid names:
Nakcheon-jeong, Apgu-jeong, Mangwon-jeong, Seonyu-jeong.

So the Han River embraces the qualities of our great and good,
our nation's ancient history,
reflects the blue sky and white clouds,
and still today flows quietly.

Miss Hassan

Perhaps it might have been in mid-January 1961?
As the bus our group was riding in
arrived outside Blenheim Palace near Oxford
people were engaged in restoring the building
like everywhere in England.

Therefore, as we got off the bus I muttered to myself,
"The English have a genius for preservation,"
At which, lo and behold, Miss Hassan, who was right behind
me,
replied in a flash: "Indeed, from preservation of property to
preservation of prejudice."

Short in stature, wearing Islamic dress,
eyes shining with intelligence,
Miss Hassan was from Lahore University in Pakistan.

If she suddenly came into my mind this morning,
after being forgotten for nearly half a century,
it was because of a news flash on the television
saying that there had been a terrorist attack in Lahore.
If she were still alive she, too, would be more than eighty,
retaining her wit and intelligence daintily in an elderly
appearance;
I hope she is still enjoying a peaceful old age.

Sword Peak

From the upstairs study in my house
I can see one pointed peak
rising at the end of a ridge extending from Mount Bukhan.

The people in my neighborhood call it Sword Peak;
the name comes perhaps from the way
it rises so precipitously.

Among the words used in the old days
to designate the belongings of an aristocrat
were "geomungo and books" and "books and swords."

But in my study I only have books,
no geomungo and no sword. Only I can see a peak
that is like the tip of a writing brush and the tip of a sword.

Greetings

Spring being exceptionally warm,
on the trees in my garden
flower-buds have early begun to swell and burst.

And on the dry bleached lawn
fresh blades of grass are sprouting green.

But what gladdens me most,
hidden at the foot of banks and walls,
are shyly peeping violets and dandelions.

To those simple friends, seen again after a year has passed,
my gaze sends affectionate greetings.

Mediterranean Observations

– August 1961

While plastic bombs were exploding in Paris,
on the sea off Algiers, early one morning,
the graceful sails of yachts were bellying with wind.

War and peace sounded like an utter hoax:
the mountain range along the African coast
lay all day under a sheet of summer haze;

and a lighthouse on the coast of Tunisia,
where another battle had broken out,
was beaming light even on that night.

Don't be surprised: 'Portuguese man-of-war'
is the name of a jellyfish, the size of a mat.
The sea was dissolving tints of blue again the next day.

Translated by Kim Jong-Gil

Suez Canal

Ship after ship passes slowly, or waits

For others to pass, on this tepid stretch
Of water, down a summer afternoon.
Nothing seems to stir: the brown, dead sands;
The sparse, dusty trees on the bank;
Not even the moving ships: everything,
Dead or asleep, endures the stifling heat
Of the sinister sun.
The only soothing green in the hushed daylight
Is this canal, rather dull, almost
Unmoving, stagnant pool of water at length:
Yet how its colour stands out in contrast
To the scene of monotonous aridness.
The blue-veined body of a monstrous moth
With vast, dried-up wings which have forgotten
To flutter for centuries;
Or a fading dream, spent of its original
Vividness, the ruthless human interest,
Which forced the channel through the hundred miles
Of sizzling sands: that is all it means
To an idle passenger on the deck of a liner,
Whose eyes are delighted at the far-away
White feluccas, the little butterflies,
Lambent over the breezy Delta.

Note: This poem, originally composed in English, was first published in the Times Literary Supplement *in 1961.*

To Seamus Heaney

We have met twice:
the first time in Cambridge;
the second in Kyoto.

In Cambridge, we just said "Hello."
But in Kyoto, we met every day for four days,
exchanging quite a lot.

Your wit and humour when you inscribed,
on the title page of your *Sweeney Astray*,
"with good wishes from Heaney Astray in Kyoto;"

Your gaze when you asked me, "How do you feel
in Japan" Yes. We were in a similar plight.
But in one thing, I may be luckier than you:

I write poems in Korean, not Japanese,
While you write in English, not Irish.

Translated by Kim Jong-Gil

On Setting Out

—To the late Pak Chaesam

That morning when your funeral ceremony
was held at Samsung Medical Center,
I had to leave Gimpo Airport for America.

Your setting out for Gongju
to be buried at the foot of a hill
and my setting out for America

both seemed so casual and in such haste
that I couldn't help wondering whether
life and death were really so different.

While I was flying over the Pacific Ocean,
thinking of you,
what skies were you flying through, I wondered?

Or were you once more shuffling precariously
down a Nagwon-dong alley,
as you used to do in your later days?

Translated by Kim Jong-Gil

About the Author

Kim Jong-Gil was born in 1926 in the region of Andong. He became a professor in the Department of English Language and Literature at Korea University in 1958. He retired in 1992. In addition to writing his own poetry in Korean and in Classical Chinese, he has published many translations into Korean of contemporary British and American poetry, and also has translated noted modern Korean poems into English.

Until his recent passing, he was one of Korea's most senior literary figures.

About the Translator

Brother Anthony of Taizé was born in 1942 in England and completed his studies in medieval and modern languages at the University of Oxford before becoming a member of the Community of Taizé (France) in 1969. Since 1980, he has been living in Korea and taught English literature in the English Department at Sogang University 1985-2007 and is now an Emeritus Professor there. He is also a Chair-Professor at Dankook University and President of the Royal Asiatic Society Korea Branch. He has published more than 40 volumes of English translations of modern Korean literature, mostly poetry, including works by Ku Sang, Ko Un, Ch'on Sang-Pyong, So Chong-Ju, Kim Yeong-Nang, Shin Kyong-Nim, Yi Si-Young, Kim Soo-bok, Ko Hyeong-ryeol, Oh Sae-young and Yi Mun-yol. He has also published a volume on the Korean Way of Tea.

He has received the Korea Times Translation Award, the Daesan Translation Award, the Korean Republic's Literary Award and the Korean PEN Translation Award for his work. He took Korean citizenship in 1994. His Korean name is An Sonjae. He received the Korean government's Award of Merit, Jade Crown class, in October 2008 for his work in promoting knowledge of Korean literature in the world. He has also been awarded an honorary MBE by Queen Elizabeth. His home page: http://anthony.sogang.ac.kr